Crock Pot Cookbook

50 Crock Pot Recipes for Healthy Families

Patrice Clark

Copyright © 2017 Patrice Clark
All rights reserved.

DEDICATION

We dedicate this book to our family,
our parents and children.

Table of Content

INTRODUCTION — 7
Why Crockpot ...? — 7

BREAKFAST RECIPES — 8
Apple and Sultana Spiced Oatmeal — 8
Luxury Blueberry Oatmeal — 9
Chocolate Orange Oatmeal — 10
Coconut and Banana Quinoa — 11
Full English Breakfast Omelette — 12
Spanish Omelette — 13
Banana Bread — 14
Coffee and Walnut Bread — 16
Moroccan Baked Eggs — 17
Huevos Rancheros — 19

LUNCH RECIPES — 20
Chicken Tikka Wraps — 20
Warming Chicken Soup — 22
Smoky Pork Chili — 23
Fish Chowder — 25
Honey and Mustard Ham — 26

Spiced Carrot, Coriander, and Lentil Soup	27
Chicken and Chorizo Paella	28
Bacon, Chicken, and Vegetable Pearl Barley Stew	30
Indonesian Chicken Curry	32
Broccoli, Bacon, and Blue Cheese Pasta	34

DINNER RECIPES — 36

Lamb Biryani	36
Chicken and Apricot Tagine	37
Beef and Stout Stew	39
Bacon Macaroni Cheese	40
BBQ Pulled Pork	41
Chinese Five Spice Beef	43
Chicken and Wild Mushroom Risotto	44
Luxury Spaghetti Bolognese	45
Cajun Gumbo	46
Ginger Pork Lettuce Cups	48

VEGETARIAN RECIPES — 49

Butternut Squash and Blue Cheese Risotto	49
Sweet Potato and Black Bean Chilli	50
Cauliflower and Sweet Potato Curry	52
Thai Green Curry	53

Kale and Cauliflower Macaroni Cheese	54
Mexican Quinoa	55
Lentil Dahl	56
Courgette and Coconut Pilaf	57
Mediterranean Vegetable Pasta	59
Tofu with Spicy Peanut Sauce	60

DESSERT RECIPES 61

Healthy Apple Crumble	62
Rhubarb Fool	64
Stuffed Apples	65
Port-Soaked Pears	66
Strawberry Rice Pudding	67
Indulgent Chocolate Fondue	68
Peanut Butter Brownies	69
Coconut Cake	70
Caribbean Pineapple	71
Conclusion	72

Introduction

Why Crockpot …?

The Crock Pot has revolutionized the way busy cooks prepare and enjoy their meals. With the option to simply place ingredients inside and let the crockpot do its magic, it means people can spend less time cooking and more time enjoying themselves.

This book aims to provide healthy, simply recipes designed for families. All cooking times are minimum amounts - feel free to leave the mixtures inside the crock pot for longer to enhance the flavor and texture.

Enjoy!

Breakfast Recipes

Apple and Sultana Spiced Oatmeal

Prep Time: 10 mins
Cooking Time: 2 hours
Serves: 4
Effort: Easy
Ingredients:

- 200g oatmeal
- 500ml almond milk
- 1 tbsp honey
- 1 tbsp cinnamon
- 1 tbsp nutmeg
- 1 cup diced apple, peeled
- 1 cup sultanas

Directions:

1. Place your crock pot on the LOW setting.
2. Place all of the ingredients into the crock pot and leave for 2 hours.
3. Serve in deep bowls with extra nutmeg to garnish.

Luxury Blueberry Oatmeal

Prep Time: 10 mins
Cooking Time: 2 hours
Serves: 4
Effort: Easy
Ingredients:

- 200g oatmeal
- 400 ml almond milk
- 100ml single cream
- 2 cups blueberries
- 2 tbsp brown sugar

Directions:

1. Place your crock pot on the LOW setting.

2. Place all of the ingredients into the crock pot and leave for 2 hours.

3. Serve in deep bowls with extra blueberries to garnish.

Chocolate Orange Oatmeal

Prep Time: 10 mins
Cooking Time: 2 hours
Serves: 4
Effort: Easy
Ingredients:

- 200g oatmeal
- 500ml almond milk
- 2 oranges, juice and zest of
- 4 squares dark chocolate
- 1 tbsp cocoa powder
- 1 tbsp money

Directions:

1. Place your crock pot on the HIGH setting.

2. Place all of the ingredients into the crock pot and leave for 2 hours.
3. Serve in deep bowls.

Coconut and Banana Quinoa

Prep Time: 10 minutes
Cooking Time: 2 hours
Serves: 4
Effort: Easy
Ingredients:

- 200g quinoa
- 400g tin of coconut milk
- 100ml almond milk
- 3 ripe bananas, mashed
- 1 tbsp honey

Directions:

1. Place your crock pot on the LOW setting.

2. Place all of the ingredients into the crock pot and leave for 2 hours.

3. Serve in deep bowls and drizzle with honey to finish.

Full English Breakfast Omelette

Prep Time: 15 minutes
Cooking Time: 2 hours
Serves: 4
Effort: Easy
Ingredients:

- **2 pork or beef sausages, cooked and sliced**
- **2 rashers of bacon**
- **6-8 chestnut mushrooms, sliced**
- **2 tomatoes, sliced**
- **10 eggs, beaten**

Directions:

1. Set the crock pot to the LOW settings.

2. In a large mixing bowl, combine all of the ingredients and transfer to the crock pot.
3. Cook for 2 hours.

Spanish Omelette

Prep Time: 15 minutes
Cooking Time: 2 hours
Serves: 4
Effort: Easy
Ingredients:

- **3 white potatoes, peels and sliced**
- **1 red pepper, sliced**
- **½ chorizo sausage, sliced**
- **1 white onion, sliced**
- **8 eggs, beaten**
- **1 tbsp smoked paprika**

Directions:

1. Set the crock pot to the LOW settings.

2. In a large mixing bowl, combine all of the ingredients and transfer to the crock pot.
3. Cook for 2 hours.

Banana Bread

Prep Time: 30 mins
Cooking Time: 2 hours
Serves: 4
Effort: Medium
Ingredients:

- 2 cups ripe bananas, mashed
- 2 eggs, beaten
- ½ cup sugar
- 2 cups plain flour
- 1 tsp baking powder
- ½ tsp baking soda
- ½ tsp salt

Directions:

1. Set your crock pot to the HIGH setting.
2. In a large mixing bowl, combine the butter and sugar until at a fluffy consistency, using either a hand-held or electric whisk.
3. Add the eggs and put to one side.
4. In another bowl, stir together the remaining ingredients. Slowly add the flour mixture to the butter and sugar mixture, folding into each other gently to form the batter.
5. Once ready, grease your crock pot with butter and pour in the batter.
6. After 2 hours, tip the pot upside down onto a cooling rack
7. Cool for 15 minutes before serving.

Coffee and Walnut Bread

Prep Time: 30 mins
Cooking Time: 2 hours
Serves: 4
Effort: Medium
Ingredients:

- 1 cup cooled black coffee
- 2 cups walnuts, crushed
- ½ cup sugar
- 2 cups plain flour
- 1 tsp baking powder
- ½ tsp baking soda
- ½ tsp salt

Directions:

1. Set your crock pot to the HIGH setting.

2. In a large mixing bowl, combine the butter and sugar until at a fluffy consistency, using either a hand-held or electric whisk.

3. Add the eggs and put to one side.

4. In another bowl, stir together the remaining ingredients. Slowly add the flour mixture to the butter and sugar mixture, folding into each other gently to form the batter.

5. Once ready, grease your crock pot with butter and pour in the batter.

6. After 2 hours, tip the pot upside down onto a cooling rack

7. Cool for 15 minutes before serving.

Moroccan Baked Eggs

Prep Time: 15 minutes
Cooking Time: 2 hours
Serves: 4

Effort: Medium
Ingredients:

- 400g tinned tomatoes
- 1 white onion, diced
- 2 garlic cloves, crushed
- 1 tsp cumin
- 1 tsp turmeric
- 1 red pepper, sliced
- 1 yellow pepper, sliced
- 1 tsp chilli flakes (optional)
- ½ cup chopped flat leaf parsley
- 8 eggs

Directions:

1. Set the slow cooker to HIGH.
2. Add all of the ingredients EXCEPT the eggs and the parsley to the crock pot and leave to cook for 2 hours.
3. Remove the lid to crack over the eggs and replace the lid for a further 10 minutes. If you refer your eggs hard, leave on for a further 15 minutes.
4. Ladle the mixture onto plates, being careful not to break the egg yolk, and scatter over the chopped

Huevos Rancheros

Prep Time: 15 mins
Cooking Time: 2.5 hours
Serves: 4
Effort: Medium
Ingredients:

- 400g tin of black beans, drained and rinsed
- ½ red chilli, deseeded and finely chopped
- ½ white onion, peeled and diced
- 400g tin of chopped tomatoes
- 2 garlic cloves, peeled and diced
- 2 ripe avocados, peeled and sliced
- ½ lime, juice of
- 1 cup fresh coriander, chopped
- 4 eggs

Directions:

1. Set your crock pot to the HIGH setting.

2. Place the onions, garlic, black beans, chopped tomatoes, and chilli into the slow cooker and leave for two hours.

3. Remove the lid to crack over the eggs and replace the lid for a further 10 minutes. If you refer your eggs hard, leave on for a further 15 minutes.

4. Ladle onto plates, arranging the sliced avocado on the side and scattering the coriander on top.

Lunch recipes

Chicken Tikka Wraps

Prep Time: 20 minutes
Cooking Time: 2 hours
Serves: 4

Effort: Easy
Ingredients:
- 4 chicken breasts, diced
- 3 tbsp chicken tikka paste
- 4 cups natural yoghurt
- 8 tortilla wraps
- ½ cup fresh mint, chopped
- ½ cup fresh coriander, chopped
- ½ cup cucumber, peeled and diced

Directions:
1. Set the crock pot to the LOW setting.
2. In a mixing bowl, combine the diced chicken breast with the tikka paste and 2 cups of yoghurt.
3. Place in the slow cooker with a drizzle of olive oil and leave for 2 hours.
4. Meanwhile, mix the remaining 2 cups of yoghurt with the herbs and cucumber.
5. Once cooked, arrange your chicken tikka in the tortilla wraps and spoon on the yoghurt mixture.

Warming Chicken Soup

Prep Time: 20 mins
Cooking Time: 3-4 hours
Serves: 4
Effort: Easy

Ingredients:

- 3 cups cooked roast chicken, sliced
- 2 celery sticks, sliced
- 1 white onion, diced
- 2 carrots, peeled and sliced
- 700ml chicken stock
- 2 nests wholewheat noodles

Directions:

1. Add all ingredients except the noodles to the slow cooker and cook for 3-4 hours on low.

2. 30 minutes before serving the soup, boil the noodles for 6-8 minutes in salted water.

3. Add the noodles to the crock pot and stir.
4. Serve the soup with crusty bread.

Smoky Pork Chili

Prep Time: 20 mins
Cooking Time: 4 hours
Serves: 4
Effort: Medium
Ingredients:

- 500g pork mince
- 2 tbsp chipotle paste
- 2 tbsp tomato puree
- 500ml chicken stock
- 1 onion, diced
- 4 spring onions, sliced
- 4 tbsp sour cream

Directions:

1. Set the crock pot to the setting LOW.
2. Add the onion, pork mince, chipotle paste, tomato puree, and chicken stock to the crock pot.
3. After 4 hours, serve in bowls topped with a dollop of sour cream and sprinkled spring onions.

Fish Chowder

Prep Time: 10 minutes
Cooking Time: 4 hours
Serves: 4
Effort: Easy
Ingredients:

- 2 cups smoked haddock, diced
- 1 cup salmon, diced
- 4 white potatoes, diced

- 2 carrots, peeled and diced
- 500ml fish stock
- 100ml double cream
- ½ cup chopped dill

Directions:

1. Set your crock pot to the LOW setting.
2. Add all of the ingredients to the vessel, except a pinch of dill for garnish.
3. Cook for 4 hours and serve with crusty bread.

Honey and Mustard Ham

Prep Time: 20 mins
Cooking Time: 3 hours
Serves: 4-6
Effort: Easy

Ingredients:
- 1 ham joint
- 1 cup runny honey
- 4 tbsp Dijon mustard
- 1 cup fresh orange juice

Directions:

1. Set the crock pot to the LOW setting.

2. Combine the honey, mustard, and orange juice in a measuring jug.

3. Place the ham joint in the crock pot and pour over the mixture.

4. Cook for 3-4 hours and serve with crusty bread, salad, and chutney.

Spiced Carrot, Coriander, and Lentil Soup

Prep Time: 20 mins
Cooking Time: 3 hours
Serves: 4
Effort: Easy
Ingredients:

- 10-12 carrots, peeled and diced
- 1 onion, diced
- 2 cups red lentils, rinsed
- 2 cups fresh coriander, chopped
- 400ml vegetable stock
- 2 tsp cumin
- 2 tsp turmeric
- 2 tsp curry powder
- 1 tsp paprika

Directions:

1. Set the crock pot to the LOW setting.
2. Place all of the ingredients into the crock pot, leaving a pinch of coriander aside for a garnish.
3. Cook for 3 hours and serve in deep bowls accompanied by crusty bread.

Chicken and Chorizo Paella

Prep Time: 30 mins
Cooking Time: 2.5 hours
Serves: 4
Effort: Medium
Ingredients:

- 2 large chicken breasts, sliced into chunks
- ½ chorizo sausage, sliced into 1cm chunks
- 1 white onion, sliced
- 4 cups paella or basmati rice
- 1 red pepper, sliced
- 2 cups frozen green peas

- 400ml chicken stock
- 1 tsp turmeric
- 2 tsp smoked paprika
- 3 tbsp tomato puree

Directions:

1. Set the crock pot to a HIGH setting.
2. Heat a medium frying pan over a medium heat and add the chorizo, onion, and chicken breast.
3. Cook for 6-8 minutes and then transfer to the crock pot.
4. Add the remaining ingredients and cook for 2.5 hours.

Bacon, Chicken, and Vegetable Pearl Barley Stew

Prep Time: 20 mins
Cooking Time: 3-4 hours
Serves: 4
Effort: Medium
Ingredients:

- 2 chicken breasts, cut into chunks
- 4 rashers of bacon, sliced
- 2 leeks, sliced
- 2 carrots, peeled and sliced
- 1 celery stick, sliced
- 2 cups frozen peas
- 2 cups pearl barley
- 500ml chicken stock

Directions:

1. Set the crock pot to the HIGH setting.
2. Heat a medium frying pan over a medium flame and add the bacon and chicken.
3. Cook for 6-8 minutes and then transfer to the crock pot, along with all of the remaining ingredients.
4. Cook for 3-4 hours before serving.

Indonesian Chicken Curry

Prep Time: 25 mins
Cooking Time: 3-4 hours
Serves: 4
Effort: Medium
Ingredients:

- 4 chicken thigh fillets, diced
- 1 white onion
- 400g coconut milk
- 1 green chilli, deseeded and diced
- 1 thumb-sized piece of ginger, crushed
- 2 garlic cloves, crushed
- 2 tbsp tomoato puree
- 1 tbsp Cayenne pepper
- 400ml chicken stock

Directions:

1. Set the crock pot to LOW.

2. Heat a medium frying pan over a medium flame and add the onions and diced chicken with a splash of oil.

3. Cook the chicken until browned, for around 5-7 minutes, and then transfer to the slow cooker.

4. Add all ingredients to the crock pot and cook for at least 4 hours.

5. Serve with boiled basmati rice.

Broccoli, Bacon, and Blue Cheese Pasta

Prep Time: 20 mins
Cooking Time: 2 hours
Serves: 4
Effort: Medium
Ingredients:

- **300g penne or fusilli pasta**
- **1 head of broccoli, cut into florets**

- 4 bacon rashers, sliced
- 1 cup blue cheese, crumbled
- 300ml whole milk
- 1 tbsp cornflour
- 1 tsp Dijon mustard

Directions:

1. Set the crock pot on the LOW setting.
2. Add all of the ingredients to the crock pot and stir thoroughly.
3. Cook for 2 hours and then serve.

Dinner Recipes

Lamb Biryani

Prep Time: 30 mins
Cooking Time: 4 hours

Serves: 4
Effort: Medium
Ingredients:

- 400g lamb, diced
- 1 onion, peeled and diced
- 1 green chilli, diced
- 2 garlic cloves, peeled and diced
- 1 thumb-sized piece of ginger, peeled and diced
- 3 cups spinach, washed
- 2 cups basmati rice
- 500ml lamb or chicken stock
- 1 tsp cumin
- 1 tsp coriander
- 1 tbsp garam masala
- 2 tbsp curry powder
- 2 cups fresh coriander, chopped

Directions:

1. Set the crock pot to LOW.
2. Heat a medium frying pan over a medium flame and add the onions and diced lamb with a splash of oil.
3. Cook the lamb until browned, for around 5-7 minutes, and then transfer to the slow cooker.
4. Add all ingredients except the fresh coriander to the crock pot and cook for at least 4 hours.
5. Serve with the fresh coriander scattered over.

Chicken and Apricot Tagine

Prep Time: 25 mins
Cooking Time: 4 hours
Serves: 4
Effort: Easy
Ingredients:

- 4 chicken thigh fillets, cut into cubes
- 1 cup dried apricots, chopped
- 1 cup black olives
- 2 beef tomatoes, cut into slices and then halved
- 1 large white onion, spiced
- 1 thumb-sized piece of ginger, peeled and chopped
- 500ml chicken stock
- 1 tbsp ras el hanout spice mixture
- 1 tsp chilli flakes
- ½ cup lemon juice

- 1 cup fresh parsley, chopped

Directions:

1. Set the slow cooker on the LOW setting.
2. Place a medium pan over a medium flame and add the onion and chicken with a splash of oil.
3. Cook for 6 minutes and then add to the slow cooker, along with all of the remaining ingredients.
4. Leave for 4 hours and serve with couscous.

Beef and Stout Stew

Prep Time: 15 minutes
Cooking Time: 4 hours
Serves: 4
Effort: Easy
Ingredients:

- 500g diced beef
- 2 white potatoes, peeled and diced
- 2 carrots, peeled and sliced

- 1 leek, sliced
- 1 celery stick, sliced
- 200ml beef stock
- 300l bottle of stout

Directions:
1. Set the crock pot to the LOW setting.
2. In a frying pan, add a splash of oil and the beef chunks.
3. Fry for 5-7 minutes, until browned, and then add to the crock pot with the remaining ingredients.
4. Cook for 4 hours and serve with mashed potato.

Bacon Macaroni Cheese

Prep Time: 5 minutes
Cooking Time: 3 hours
Serves: 4
Effort: Extra easy
Ingredients:

- 4 cups grated cheddar
- 6 cups dried macaroni pasta
- 2 cups full-fat milk
- 2 cans evaporated milk
- 1 tsp Dijon mustard
- 2 bacon rashers

Directions:

1. Set the crock pot on the LOW setting.
2. Add all of the ingredients to the crock pot and stir thoroughly.
3. Cook for 3 hours and then serve.

BBQ Pulled Pork

Prep Time: 15 mins
Cooking Time: 5 hours

Serves: 8
Effort: Medium
Ingredients:

- 1.5-2kg pork shoulder
- 150ml apple cider vinegar
- 150ml chicken stock
- 200ml BBQ sauce
- 1 cup brown sugar
- 1 tsp mustard
- 1 tsp Worcestershire sauce
- 1 tsp chilli powder
- 2 garlic cloves
- 1 white onion, peeled and sliced

Directions:

1. Set the crock pot to the high settings.
2. Combine all of the ingredients, except the pork shoulder joint, in the crock pot.
3. Place the joint into the slow cooker and rotate to ensure its covered in the mixture.
4. Cook for 5 hours and then serve in baps.

Chinese Five Spice Beef

Prep Time: 15 mins
Cooking Time: 4 hours
Serves: 4
Effort: Medium
Ingredients:

- 600g beef brisket
- 2 tbsp Chinese Five Spice powder
- 400ml beef stock
- 2 garlic cloves, crushed
- 1 piece thumb-sized ginger, sliced
- 1 red chilli, deseeded and diced
- 1 bunch pak choi, sliced

Directions:

1. Set the crock pot to the HIGH setting.

2. Add all of the ingredients to the vessel and cook for 4 hours.

3. Serve with rice.

Chicken and Wild Mushroom Risotto

Prep Time: 20 mins
Cooking Time: 3 hours
Serves: 4
Effort: Medium
Ingredients:
- 4 chicken breasts, sliced
- 2 tbsp dried porcini mushrooms
- 4 cups risotto rice
- 1 cup creme fraiche
- 600ml chicken stock
- 2 garlic cloves
- 1 white onion, diced
- 1 cup white wine
- 1 cup fresh parsley, chopped

Directions:

1. Set the slow cooker to the HIGH setting.
2. In a frying pan over a medium heat, fry the chicken, garlic, and onions with a splash of oil for 5 minutes.
3. Transfer this to the crock pot and add all of the remaining ingredients, except the fresh parsley.
4. Serve sprinkled with fresh parsley after 3 hours of cooking time.

Luxury Spaghetti Bolognese

Prep Time: 20 mins
Cooking Time: 4 hours
Serves: 4
Effort: Easy
Ingredients:

- 500g beef mince, 10% fat or less
- 2 rashers of bacon, sliced

- ½ chorizo, sliced
- 1 white onion, sliced
- 2 garlic cloves, peeled and chopped
- 400g tin of tomatoes
- 1 tbsp Worcestershire sauce
- 1 tbsp tomato puree
- 1 tsp mixed herbs
- 1 cup fresh basic, chopped

Directions:

1. Set the crock pot to the LOW setting.
2. Over a medium heat, fry the garlic, minced beef, and onion for 5 minutes until browned.
3. Then, transfer all of the ingredients to the crock pot and let cook for four hours.
4. Serve with cooked spaghetti and garlic bread.

Cajun Gumbo

***Prep Time:* 25 mins**
***Cooking Time:* 5 hours**
***Serves:* 4**
Effort: Medium
Ingredients:

- 2 chicken breasts, sliced into chunks
- 2 cups king prawns
- 1 red pepper, sliced
- 1 green pepper, sliced
- 1 cup sweet corn, drained
- 1 white onion, sliced
- 2 beef tomatoes, cut into chunks
- 1 tbsp Cajun seasoning
- 1 tbsp Cayenne pepper
- 500ml chicken stock

Directions:

1. Place the crock pot on the LOW setting.
2. Add all of the ingredients to the crock pot and allow to cook for 5 hours.
3. Serve with rice.

Ginger Pork Lettuce Cups

Prep Time: 30 mins
Cooking Time: 3 hours
Serves: 4
Effort: Medium
Ingredients:

- 400g pork mince
- 1 thumb-sized piece of ginger
- 2 garlic cloves
- 1 tbsp Chinese five spice
- 200ml chicken stock
- 1 carrot, diced into small pieces
- 1 cup water chestnuts, diced
- 12 lettuce leaves, washed

Directions:
1. Set the crock pot to the HIGH setting.

2. Add all of the ingredients, except the lettuce leaves, to the pot and allow to cook for 5 hours.

3. Serve warm in the lettuce leaves.

Vegetarian Recipes

Butternut Squash and Blue Cheese Risotto

Prep Time: 30 mins
Cooking Time: 3 hours
Serves: 4
Effort: Medium
Ingredients:

- 1 butternut squash, peeled, deseeded, and diced into 1cm chunks

- 1 red onion, sliced
- 200g risotto rice
- 1 cup white wine
- 500ml vegetable stock
- 2 cups stilton, crumbled
- ½ cup lemon juice

Directions:

1. Place the crock pot on the LOW setting.
2. On a baking tray, place the butternut squash and red onion and drizzle with oil.
3. After cooking for 20 minutes at 180C, add these ingredients to the crock pot.
4. Add all of the ingredients to the crock pot and allow to cook for 3 hours.

Sweet Potato and Black Bean Chilli

Prep Time: 15 mins

Cooking Time: 4 hours

Serves: 4

Effort: Easy

Ingredients:

- 400g tin black beans, drained and rinsed
- 2 large sweet potatoes, peeled and diced into 1cm chunks
- 1 can sweetcorn, drained
- 1 red pepper, sliced
- 400g can tinned tomatoes
- 1 tsp cumin
- 1 tsp turmeric
- 1 tsp chilli powder
- 2 tbsp tomato puree

Directions:

1. Place the crock pot on the LOW setting.
2. Add all of the ingredients to the crock pot and allow to cook for 4 hours.
3. Serve with rice.

Cauliflower and Sweet Potato Curry

***Prep Time:* 20 minutes**
***Cooking Time:* 4 hours**
***Serves:* 4**
***Effort:* Easy**
Ingredients:

- 1 large cauliflower, sliced into florets
- 1 large sweet potato, peeled and diced
- 400g tin chickpeas, drained and rinsed
- 400g tin coconut milk
- 1 red chilli, sliced and deseeded
- 1 cup frozen peas
- 1 tbsp turmeric
- 1 tbsp cumin

Directions:

1. Place the crock pot on the LOW setting.
2. Add all of the ingredients to the crock pot and allow to cook for 4 hours.

3. Serve with rice.

Thai Green Curry

Prep Time: 20 minutes
Cooking Time: 3 hours
Serves: 4
Effort: Medium
Ingredients:

- **2 cups sugar snap peas**
- **2 cups tender stem brocolli**
- **1 aubergine**

Directions:

1. Place the crock pot on the LOW setting.
2. Add all of the ingredients to the crock pot and allow to cook for 3 hours.

3. Serve with rice.

Kale and Cauliflower Macaroni Cheese

Prep Time: 20 minutes
Cooking Time: 3 hours
Serves: 4
Effort: Medium
Ingredients:

- 300g macaroni pasta
- 300ml whole milk
- 1 can evaporated milk
- 3 cups grated cheddar
- 1 cauliflower, cut into florets
- 3 cups kale, washed and shredded

Directions:

1. Place the crock pot on the LOW setting.

2. Add all of the ingredients to the crock pot and allow to cook for 3 hours.

Mexican Quinoa

Prep Time: 20 mins
Cooking Time: 3 hours
Serves: 4
Effort: Easy
Ingredients:

- 400g can of black beans
- 200g can of sweetcorn
- 4 spring onions, sliced
- 4 tomatoes, diced
- 400g tin chopped tomatoes
- 2 avocados, peeled and diced
- 2 cups fresh coriander, chopped
- 1 lime, juice of

Directions:

1. Place the crock pot on the LOW setting.
2. Add all of the ingredients, except the avocado and coriander, to the crock pot and allow to cook for 3 hours.
3. Once served, add the avocado and coriander to the top.

Lentil Dahl

Prep Time: 20 minutes
Cooking Time: 4 hours
Serves: 4
Effort: Medium
Ingredients:

- 400g yellow lentils
- 500ml vegetable stock
- 1 tbsp cumin
- 1 tbsp turmeric
- 1 tsp fennel seeds

- 400g tin of coconut milk
- 1 green chilli, deseeded and diced
- 2 cups fresh coriander, chopped

Directions:

1. Place the crock pot on the LOW setting.
2. Add all of the ingredients to the crock pot and allow to cook for 4 hours.
3. Serve with rice or naan.

Courgette and Coconut Pilaf

Prep Time: 20 minutes
Cooking Time: 3 hours
Serves: 4
Effort: Easy
Ingredients:

- 2 courgettes, diced into 1cm chunks

- 1 white onion, peeled and diced
- 2 garlic cloves, peeled and sliced
- 1 tsp ground coriander
- 1 tsp fennels seeds
- 1 tbsp cumin
- 1 tsp turmeric
- 1 cinnamon stick
- 500ml vegetable stock
- 1 cup desiccated coconut, toasted

Directions:

1. Place the crock pot on the HIGH setting.
2. Add all of the ingredients to the crock pot and allow to cook for 3 hours.

Mediterranean Vegetable Pasta

Prep Time: 20 mins

Cooking Time: 2 hours
Serves: 4
Effort: Medium
Ingredients:

- 1 large red pepper, sliced
- 1 red onion, sliced
- 1 courgette, sliced
- 1 aubergine, cubed
- 300g fusilli or penne pasta
- 400g tinned tomatoes
- 1 cup fresh basil, chopped

Directions:

1. Set the crock pot to the HIGH setting.
2. Add all of the ingredients to the pot and cook for 2 hours.

Tofu with Spicy Peanut Sauce

Prep Time: 20 mins
Cooking Time: 4.5 hours
Serves: 4
Effort: Medium
Ingredients:

- 600g firm tofu
- 1 cup peanut butter
- 1 cup soy sauce
- 2 garlic cloves, crushed
- 1 tbsp crushed red chill
- 2 tbsp sesame oil
- 1 lime, juice of
- 1 tbsp brown sugar

Directions:

1. Combine all of the ingredients except the tofu in the slow cooker and mix thoroughly.
2. Set the crock pot to the LOW setting.
3. Add the tofu and cook for 4.5 hours.
4. Serve with steamed rice and broccoli.

Dessert Recipes

Vanilla PoachedPeaches

Prep Time: 15 mins
Cooking Time: 1.5 hours
Serves: 4
Effort: Easy
Ingredients:

- 8 peaches, scored along the bottom
- 500ml sweet white wine
- 2 tbsp brown sugar
- 1 vanilla pod

Directions:

1. Set the crock pot to the LOW setting.
2. Mix all ingredients except the peaches in the vessel.
3. Add the peaches and cook for 1.5 hours.
4. Serve with vanilla ice cream.

Healthy Apple Crumble

Prep Time: 30 mins
Cooking Time: 3.5 hours
Serves: 4
Effort: Medium
Ingredients:

- **6 cooking apples, peeled, cored and diced**
- **1 tbsp cinnamon**
- **1 cup sultanas**
- **1 cup honey**
- **200ml water**
- **4 cups oats**
- **1 cup brown sugar**
- **1 tsp nutmeg**

Directions:

1. Set the crock pot to the LOW setting and add the apples, cinnamon, sultanas, honey, and water.

2. Leave to cook for 3 hours.

3. Meanwhile, mix the oats, brown sugar, and nutmeg in a mixing bowl.

4. Once the apples are cooked, transfer to a baking dish and top with the oat mixture.

5. Grill for 20-30 minutes and then serve.

Rhubarb Fool

Prep Time: 20 mins
Cooking Time: 2.5 hours
Serves: 4
Effort: Easy
Ingredients:

- **10 sticks of fresh rhubarb, sliced into 1cm pieces**
- **1 cup brown sugar**
- **200ml water**
- **400ml double cream**
- **4 meringue nests, crushed**

Directions:

1. Set the crock pot to the LOW setting.
2. Add the rhubarb, sugar, and water all allow to cook for 2.5 hours.
3. Meanwhile, use an electric whisk to thicken the double cream.
4. Once the rhubarb has cooled, combine with the cream and meringue and serve topped with fresh mint.

Stuffed Apples

Prep Time: 20 mins
Cooking Time: 2 hours
Serves: 4

Effort: Medium
Ingredients:
- 4 red apples, cored
- 2 cups oatmeal
- 1 tbsp cinnamon
- 1 tbsp butter
- 1 cup honey
- 150ml water

Directions:
1. Set the crock pot to LOW.
2. In a mixing bowl, combine the oats with the cinnamon, butter, and honey.
3. Stuff the apples with the mixture and then pour the water into the crock pot before placing the apples inside.
4. Cook for 2 hours and serve with cream.

Port-Soaked Pears

Prep Time: 10 minutes
Cooking Time: 2 hours

Serves: 4
Effort: Easy
Ingredients:

- 4 large, ripe pears
- 400ml ruby port
- 1 cup caster sugar
- 2 tbsp lemon juice

Directions:

1. Set the crock pot to HIGH.
2. Combine the port with the caster sugar and lemon juice and transfer to the crock pot.
3. Add the pears, sideways down, and cook for 2 hours.
4. Serve with double cream.

Strawberry Rice Pudding

Prep Time: 10 minutes
Cooking Time: 2.5 hours

Serves: 6
Effort: Easy
Ingredients:

- 150g short-grain rice
- 800ml milk
- 200ml double cream
- 1 tbsp nutmeg
- 3 cups strawberries, chopped

Directions:

1. Set the crock to the HIGH setting.
2. Add all the ingredients to the vessel and cook for 2.5 hours.

Indulgent Chocolate Fondue

Prep Time: 10 minutes
Cooking Time: 1 hour
Serves: 6

***Effort:** Easy*
Ingredients:
- 250ml double cream
- 350g plain chocolate, chopped
- 1 tsp vanilla extract

Directions:
1. Place all ingredients in the slow cooker and set it to LOW.
2. Cook for 1 hour and serve with strawberries, marshmallows, and nuts for dipping.

Peanut Butter Brownies

***Prep Time:** 20 minutes*
***Cooking Time:** 2.5 hours*
***Serves:** 6*
***Effort:** Easy*
Ingredients:
- ½ cup melted butter

- 1 cup cocoa powder
- 1 cup plain flour
- 2 tbsp smooth peanut butter
- 2 eggs
- 2 cups chocolate chips
- 2 tbsp honey

Directions:

1. Line the crock pot with parchment paper and set to HIGH.
2. Combine the ingredients in a mixing bowl and add to the crock pot.
3. Cook for 2 hours and then serve.

Coconut Cake

Prep Time: 20 minutes
Cooking Time: 2.5 hours

Serves: 6
Effort: Medium
Ingredients:

- 1 cup self-raising flour
- 1 tsp baking soda
- 1 tsp baking powder
- 2 cups brown sugar
- 4 eggs, beaten
- 2 cups dessicated coconut
- 1 tsp vanilla extract

Directions:

1. Line the crock pot with baking parchment and set to HIGH.
2. Combine all ingredients in a mixing bowl and cook for 2 hours.

Caribbean Pineapple

Prep Time: 10 minutes
Cooking Time: 2.5 hours
Serves: 6
Effort: Easy
Ingredients:

- 1 large pineapple, peeled and cut into chunks
- 2 cups rum
- 1 cup brown sugar

Directions:

1. Set the crock pot to HIGH.
2. Combine all ingredients and cook for 2 hours.
3. Serve with ice crea.

Thanks for downloading this book.
It is my firm belief that it has provided you with all the answers to your questions.